T0195918

In The Last Days

And If You Find Yourself Still Here

I V O N N E   O .   P Y K E

WESTBOW
PRESS®
A DIVISION OF THOMAS NELSON
& ZONDERVAN

This book is a work of non-fiction. Unless otherwise noted, the author and the publisher make no explicit guarantees as to the accuracy of the information contained in this book and in some cases, names of people and places have been altered to protect their privacy.

WestBow Press books may be ordered through booksellers or by contacting:

WestBow Press
A Division of Thomas Nelson & Zondervan
1663 Liberty Drive
Bloomington, IN 47403
www.westbowpress.com
844-714-3454

Because of the dynamic nature of the Internet, any web addresses or links contained in this book may have changed since publication and may no longer be valid. The views expressed in this work are solely those of the author and do not necessarily reflect the views of the publisher, and the publisher hereby disclaims any responsibility for them.

Any people depicted in stock imagery provided by Getty Images are models, and such images are being used for illustrative purposes only. Certain stock imagery © Getty Images.

Interior Image Credit: Image by Calvary Chapel Perth, Austrailia. Used by permission

Scripture quotations are taken from the NEW AMERICAN STANDARD BIBLE®, Copyright © 1960, 1962, 1963, 1968, 1971, 1972, 1973, 1975, 1977, 1995, 2020 by The Lockman Foundation. Used by permission. As presented in the NASB Thinline Bible (2020 Text), published by Zondervan, 2021, all rights reserved

Scripture quotations marked (NKJV) are taken from the New King James Version. Copyright © 1982 by Thomas Nelson, Inc. Used by permission. All rights reserved.

Scripture quotations marked KJV are taken from the King James Version, public domain.

ISBN: 979-8-3850-1571-9 (sc)
ISBN: 979-8-3850-1570-2 (e)

Library of Congress Control Number: 2023924633

Print information available on the last page.

WestBow Press rev. date: 02/13/2024

In loving memory of my *abuela*, who taught me so much, and my brother/best friend, who passed away before we could carry out our best plans to change the trajectory of our family. Until we meet again.

Preface

I thank my Lord and Savior, Jesus Christ, for helping me write something that has never been on my radar. I thank Him for helping me overcome domestic violence, survive cancer, and a host of other obstacles. He isn't finished with me yet. Praise be the name of the Lord! #Psalm100

Introduction

There are different viewpoints about the exact timeline or sequence of events for the end-times. There are those who believe in the pretribulation Rapture of believers/followers of Jesus Christ—meaning that the Rapture of the church will take place before any of the seven years of tribulation. There are those who believe in midtribulation—meaning that the Rapture will take place midway through the tribulation, which will be at the end of the first three and a half years. And there are those who believe in post-tribulation—meaning the Rapture will take place at the end of the seven years of tribulation.

The church of true believers is the "bride of Christ." We can read about this in Matthew 25:1–13, Revelation 19:7–8, and Revelation 21:1–2. It is the belief and viewpoint of this author that the Rapture of the church (those who have accepted Jesus Christ as their personal Lord and Savior) comes before the tribulation.

The Rapture will take place just like a thief comes in the night. Jesus will come for His valuables. The tribulation will be a hard, dark time. It will get worse as time passes. The Lord is the groom of the church. Think of a bride and all she does to prepare for her wedding. A bride plans and purposefully dresses for the occasion. In doing so, the bride wants to look her best for the groom. It is an anticipated time to remember. I can't recall a groom ever dragging his bride through the mud, so to speak, before such an important event. What bride has ever stood at the altar looking worn, torn, and dirty from horrible events before their wedding?

The Bible says this wedding supper of the Lamb is a greatly awaited occasion for which the bride makes herself ready.

> And I heard, as it were, the voice of a great multitude, as the sound of many waters and as the sound of mighty peals of thunder, saying, "Hallelujah! For the Lord our God, the Almighty, reigns. Let us rejoice and be glad and give glory to Him, for the marriage of the Lamb has come and His bride has made herself ready." And it was given to her to clothe herself in fine linen, bright and clean;—for the fine linen is the righteous acts of the saints. And he said to me, "Write, 'Blessed are those who are invited to the marriage supper of the Lamb.'" And he said to me, "These are the true words of God." (Revelation 19:6–9, NASB)

All through the Bible, one can read about the great lengths God goes through to show His love. This amount of love and forgiveness is more than we can ever produce ourselves. The Bible speaks of God numbering the hairs on our heads (Luke

12:7). We are in the palms of His hands (Isaiah 49:16). In the New Testament book of Matthew, we read that we are worth more than the sparrows (Matthew 10:31). John 3:16 talks about God loving us so much that He sent His only Son—His only child! God makes many more points in scriptures to show His love for us. To follow suit with His level of love, preparedness, and care, this author believes His investment of the bride's wedding preparation will be proper and valued.

Around the Corner

As a child, I heard a preacher speak passionately about Heaven and Hell. One thing he said really spoke to my seven-year-old self. He said that sin could not enter Heaven. So God sent His only Son to come to the earth born of a virgin, Mary. He would grow up in human form to experience what we do and eventually pay the price needed to take our sins away. That price was hefty. He died in our place as a sacrifice and payment for past, present, and future sins so we could be together in Heaven. He was willing to be beaten, spit on, mocked, and whipped with flesh-tearing weapons for me and you!

Now as a seven-year-old, I was looking with eyes wide open at this preacher. I was aware of what spankings were and how much they hurt. So I was thinking, *Wow! He took a whipping in* my *place and spared me* all that pain! It suddenly became real to me. He did it all because He loves me and wants to be with me. He paid the price for *me*. That Sunday night, I gave my heart and my life to Jesus Christ.

Fast-forward to several decades, through an acquaintance, I heard about the Voice of the Martyrs and how there are countries where people are being punished, tortured, and abused for believing and sharing Jesus as I do. So I began praying for requests marked on a calendar I purchased from their website. It contained a country per day and a small sentence of their prayer needs. While walking my dog, the idea came to me that I needed to write a small book to make mention of some coming events of the end-times. I asked the Lord to help me write about them.

I asked the Lord to help me explain the game of smoke and mirrors that the devil likes to play. When I say smoke and mirrors, I'm referring to deceptive perception, trickery, and lies. For example, many years ago, the carnival used to have a fun house, which contained a maze of mirrors, making it hard to navigate. There were also mirrors that humorously distorted your reflection by causing you to look abnormally tall, short, skinny, or fat. People found it very amusing to go through the fun house.

Often, our perception can become distorted by listening to lies and believing deception. In the last days mentioned in the Bible, this will be a real issue to face. People will be deceived and believe lies. See Bible references 1 Timothy 4:1–2, 2 Corinthians 11:13–15, and 2 Thessalonians 2:3.

Faith and fear have something in common. The two of them ask you to believe something you cannot see.

As the world seems to get worse, many experience anxiety, fear, and insecurity. One main issue I want to highlight is fear. In these last days, people are treating others in ways that stem from their anxieties, fears, and insecurities. One way they do that is being mean and unfair toward others who do not think or believe as they do. This is how persecution begins. There are political persecution, racial persecution, and religious persecution. There are more, but today I want to talk about the persecution of religious beliefs and the fear felt by those who are the recipients of it or threatened by it.

The devil uses fear in different ways. Here are a few:

1. What will others think or say about me?
2. Will I lose my friends?
3. Will I lose my job?
4. Will someone hurt me because I am a Christian?
5. I think dying or threatening to kill me because I am a Christian is scary.
6. Will my loved ones reject me because of my faith?
7. Will someone cause pain or harm to my loved ones because of my faith?

Let's look past the fear tactics for a second. Instantly, I think back to the Christmas movie that has a grumpy character who hates Christmas and wants to steal it. I think most of you know who I'm talking about, right? Do you remember the part where the little girl finds his hideout in the mountains where he lives alone? She stands unaffected by the creature's several fake lunges to scare her away. If only we could have her perspective when it comes to the devil's scare tactics of fear and intimidation when, in all actuality, the devil can't do anything without God's permission. Two examples will be the stories of Job (Job 1:6–22) and Simon Peter at the Last Supper (Luke 22:31).

Now that we know the created devil is limited by the Creator, it sheds a light on what he can and cannot do. Here are some other fear tactics that he tries:

- Fear of opinions/disapproval of others
- Fear of pain
- Fear of using your loved ones against you
- Fear of loss of position, possessions, or dignity
- Fear of dying
- Fear of leaving family behind

Former US President Franklin D. Roosevelt once said, "Courage is not the absence of fear, but rather the assessment that something else is more important than fear" (Quotespedia.org).

Fear of opinions or disapproval of others—You get to choose your thoughts. You get to choose which ones you will accept or dismiss. You can decide that the Lord's opinion of you is more important than regular people's. Psalm 139:14 reminds us we are fearfully and wonderfully made. Luke 12:7 teaches us even the very hairs of our head are all numbered. Isaiah 49:16 reveals to us that He has inscribed you on the palms of His hands. If God thinks you are special, that is the only opinion that counts.

Fear of pain—It is a natural human tendency to not want to go through excessive pain and discomfort (Psalm 118:6, Matthew 10:28). When Jesus was in the Garden of Gethsemane before the crucifixion, He prayed to the point where His sweat had drops of blood in it. He knew what was ahead. Taking the beatings and the mockery in our place was hefty. That hurt.

That really hurt. Out of love, He continued with the plan to die on the cross, rise from the dead on the third day, and conquer death, Hell, and the grave. That paid for everyone's sins—past, present, *and* future. It was hard, but He made the choice. He made it a gift that must be *accepted*.

Believe that He is able to do this for you. *Confess* you cannot do anything to pay for it yourself and that Jesus is the only way. We need to make a choice. We can do something to show love back to Him, even if it causes pain.

Fear of using loved ones against you—This is a psychological and emotional way to use leverage in the devil's favor. The devil can hope that maybe love for family or friends can work against you. He hopes to persuade you to renounce Christ just to avoid seeing your loved ones suffer hardship. A choice is required. Above all, the best choice is always Christ—always and every time. The Lord will take care of your loved ones. Matthew 28:20 (KJV) says, "I will be with you always, even to the end of the world. Amen."

Fear of loss of position, possessions, or dignity—The loss of position or possessions is hard for some people. Some people work all their lives trying to gain status and acquire possessions. In all reality, though, it is just property, which cannot follow you into Heaven. Losing possessions should be addressed objectively. What will last? Store up treasures in Heaven. What are treasures? It is giving to those who cannot repay, as well as giving to charities and church. Although money is a tool, treasures are linked not just to money but also to your heart (Matthew 6:19–21).

Look at it as an exchange for an upgrade. Your dignity is separate. To be humiliated is terrible any way you look at it. Others suffer from low self-esteem, and taking away dignity will be devastating. Some suffer from pride, and taking dignity away will be equally devastating. At this point, it will be a battle inside the mind itself, so you will need to have focus. Focus on the Lord and use His quiet example. The Lord sees it all, and He will bless you in ways you cannot imagine. People may try to humiliate you, but they will not be able to take your dignity. The fear of *that*, my friend, is more fun house smoke and mirrors.

Fear of death—The *Lord* promises special rewards for those who are persecuted for His name's sake (Matthew 5:10–12). The apostle Paul says in Philippians 1:21 (KJV), "For me to live is Christ, and to die is gain." We also read in 2 Corinthians 5:8 about his confidence being absent from the body and being present with the Lord. We are in the last days, so we need to be brave.

You can do it while afraid, but resolve to stand for Jesus. You may shake or tremble, or you may be a very steady person—it is always right to stand for our Lord and Savior, Jesus Christ. Some people have a wave of courage to overcome them, and they are strong and determined and can persevere. Others feel an onset of fear, but after processing it a little, they venture forward and pray as they proceed. There will be some who feel the cost is not worth the pain and all that accompanies it.

One can only suppose what to do until it *really* happens. We want to think we won't turn our backs on the One who gave His life for us. He counted the cost, and we were worth it.

Those who are tortured for Christ must be the ones to endure to the end.

Believe in the *Lord* when He says He will reward you. You may not be able to comprehend the level of that reward simply because you do not have anything to refer it against. The cost and worth of going through anything for the *Lord* will be greatly rewarded. You never suffer loss for the *Lord*. He will see to it that you come out ahead. Matthew 5:44 compels you to love your enemies and bless those who curse you. The key is to remember and rehearse the truths in scriptures.

Fear of leaving family—Dying and leaving family behind seems scary. You need to understand that God knows the end from the beginning and that provisions are already in place. You just need to believe it. Your family members are His before they are yours. Nothing takes God by surprise, and He is always in control *always and every time*. The following verses in the Bible can be read: Isaiah 46:10, Ecclesiastes 3:11, Deuteronomy 31:8, Psalm 73:26, and Psalm 125:1–2.

Another perspective to consider during these end-times is that Christians will receive persecution from other church attenders. There are those who are set in their ways. If God moves outside those ways, then judgment, criticism, and, yes, even persecution will come from those people. This reminds me of the religious group in the Bible that didn't like the healing and hope that Jesus was giving many people. It was outside their religious rituals.

Currently, I am interested in finding out if fasting and praying for a specific time is a denominational matter or personal. Fasting is when you delay or go without food for a specific time while you seek the Lord fervently in prayer for an important need or issue. So far, I have been surprised to find that some conversations have led me to realize some churches have never fasted.

There are several ways to fast. Depending on your health, some delay a meal and use that time to pray. There are those who do the Daniel fast. (In the book of Daniel, he ate fruit, vegetables, and water. But if you search the internet for the Daniel fast, you will find that whole grains and other items are permissible too.) Then there are those who go without food completely. The amount of time you do this is up to the person. Some do a three-day fast, while others do more.

I have participated in the Daniel fast for a twenty-one-day period. Fasting is not only healthy for your body but also a time where you can experience a breakthrough in what you have been asking the Lord for in prayer. Some have never heard of fasting, and others have heard of it but see it more of a hardship than a benefit. My concern is if someone isn't willing to do the minimum and delay eating a meal, then how will they sustain the inconvenience of persecution for Christ's sake? Persecution can come from different places—and some are more shocking than others.

Psalm 35 is a chapter in the Bible that speaks about persecution. It is educationally and beautifully written. As Christ suffered verbal and physical persecution, we could face that as well. Remember to separate your feelings of the moment with the facts that are true in God's Word. Rehearsing them or even committing them to memory will keep your focus on the Lord. Praising Him in the pain of the moment will glorify Him, and the grace to bear it all will be a blessing in return. This will seem like a very odd time to be singing; however, the valuable part I want you to know is that the enemy cannot stand to be around anyone who is praising the Lord.

I've heard a preacher describe once that praise drowns out the presence of evil spirits by welcoming the Holy Spirit to come closer and angels to go into action. It's worth a shot. Try to sing a song during a very bad time (even if it is sung in your head or in a soft whisper). It is the mind that needs training to be strong in the Lord. Where the mind goes, you will follow.

As a Christian, you are asked to trust God, but can God trust you with the burden of hardship? Blessings are easy to accept, but you can't have a "blessings only" life. Can God trust you with hardship, even if it means your life is on the line? In the book of Esther, as queen, she had to make a tough decision as even her life was on the line. She was put in a unique position "for such a time as this." So if you were put in a position where you were persecuted—perhaps even if your life was on the line—you would also have a choice "for such a time as this." Can God trust you not to compromise or take the easy way out?

Thoughts of compromise are not of God. That is an unclean spirit that you need to verbally rebuke immediately in Jesus's name. Ask the Holy Spirit to help you. He has given you authority to speak against it (Luke 10:19), so use it. The whisper of compromise, gone unchecked, will only grow louder in persuasion. Spot that devil! Don't allow fear to persuade you.

Take into consideration everything that the Lord Jesus has gone through on the cross without compromise. There are preparations He has made in Heaven to be with you. It is like you are sandwiched in between two very deep acts of love.

There is nothing to truly fear. First John 4:18 (KJV) says, "There is no fear in love; but perfect love casteth out fear: because fear has torment. He that feareth is not made perfect in love." Teach us, oh Lord, how not to fear!

So how does one simply not fear? Well, take riding a bike for example. Don't fall; it will hurt. How do you not fall? What is the process of not falling? Some of the falls are going to happen because you haven't learned the process. You develop focus and balance. Whether you realize it or not, you are making mental choices. Don't lean too far this way or that way. Keep your eyes forward to where you want to go. Pedal with your feet but not too fast or too slow. Keep your hands on the handlebars. Adjust the handlebars to where you need to go. You are making choices. So how does one not fear? What is the process? What are the choices?

Mentally, you are making choices. You are weighing things out in your mind. *Is this going to hurt? Is this worth the effort? Will I stand to gain or lose something?* You measure cost and worth in your mind. *What's this going to cost me? Will it be worth it?*

Our measuring capabilities are limited. In the Bible, we read about the rewards in Heaven. There are promises made to us about being rewarded. What are God's rewards, and how do we measure the cost/worth of it? All we can do is suppose the grandeur of it all because we have no system of measurement for it. None of us have seen heavenly rewards yet. It's going to require faith and trust in God that He is not in the bait-and-switch business. Words like *abundance, extra,* and *overflowing* describe the generosity of God in the Bible. So by that, we trust rewards are more than our minds can imagine. Instead of focusing on what we may lose, focus on what we stand to gain. Focus on the doughnut, not the doughnut hole. Gifts from kings are generous.

When facing scary, fearful circumstances, stop and identify it. Point out what is making you scared or fearful. Verbally identify it. What about the scary part? Can that really happen? Even if it does, do you think God is not watching? Nothing surprises God. He is in control—always. He has done miracles for people in the Bible, so He can for you too. Analyze this: Where is your focus? Where is your balance? What process are you following?

Two big fear busters are prayer and praise. It is amazing how praise and prayer shift your focus to God. This helps so much (1 Thessalonians 5:18). It takes practice. Perfecting the skills requires repetition. You won't feel like you are good at it at first. It may even seem odd to you, but the more you do it, the better you'll get. One day fear won't have the same effect on you as it once has.

Focus, determination, perseverance. Your faith and what you believe in must mean something to you—deep seated in you. God promises to never leave us nor forsake us (Deuteronomy 31:6). He is the Creator, not a created thing. He has a plan and purpose for everything. Nothing happens without God's permission. God has created all things (Colossians 1:16). He can take bad things that happen and make something good come out of it (Romans 8:28). People have asked, "How could a God ...?" or "Why would a God ...?" And somehow in that whole line of questioning the devil is omitted. The devil is not blamed nor highlighted for his part in any of their complaints or accusations. Deep down, there is an acknowledgment of God's superiority over all things. There are some questions that cannot be answered on the earth, but we will understand them in Heaven.

Are you going? There is only *one* way: believe in the Lord Jesus Christ. He has died on the cross and paid our sin debt. Romans 3:10 lets us know that there is no one righteous, not one. Being a good enough person doesn't make us righteous. He has died on the cross, and His blood has been shed for past, present, and future sins. He has risen from the grave on the third day and will come again for those who have accepted His gift of salvation.

Those who feel they don't need it or reject it completely will be left behind on the earth to face the end of the world. After that is the judgment. Every knee will bow, and every tongue will confess that Jesus is Lord (Philippians 2:10–11). Those who have accepted Jesus's gift of salvation are saved, and their names are written down in the Book of Life (Revelation 20:15). Those whose names are not found in the Book of Life will be condemned to Hell for all eternity with no opportunity of relief or escape. The choice is yours. You can believe it or not. Once you die, your chances to decide are gone. Make your choice today before it's too late. You can pray this simple prayer:

> Father, thank You for sending Your only Son, Jesus Christ, to pay my sin debt on the cross. Jesus, thank You for dying for me and loving me that much. Thank You for rising from the dead on the third day and overcoming death, Hell, and the grave. I admit I am a sinner and need You as I cannot pay for my sins myself. I accept Your gift of salvation. I give my heart and life to You. I believe in You. In Jesus's name, I pray. Amen.

If you've prayed that prayer with all sincerity, your name has been written in the Lamb's Book of Life. Angels are rejoicing in Heaven (Luke 15:10)! Please find a Bible-believing church in your area and share your good news for the next steps!

The Lord says in Isaiah 43:1 (NASB), in the latter part of the verse, "Do not fear, for I have redeemed you; I have called you by name; you are Mine!" What a great thing to know we belong to Him unconditionally! We are His children.

I have seen a social media meme once that A. W. Tozer said, "We operate by faith, which means that we have confidence in what God says, whether we fully understand it or not." In many Bibles, there is a place in the back that has a list of verses for each topic. There, you will be able to find several verses that will tell you what God says about many things. For example, under *fear* is a list several verses that talk about that subject.

It is always a good idea to take a little bit of time and look something up that is particularly relevant to the season you are in or to just gain knowledge about the topic. Learning what the Bible says will help you recall the truths you will need to lean on and trust in when things go wrong.

We greatly err not knowing the scriptures. There are over three hundred verses in the Bible that talk about fear. We can read one every day if we want. Let God take care of it since He can do way more than we ever can, right?

The enemy is not in control of tomorrow; only God is. God is in control of today, tomorrow, and the future. Living for Jesus and telling others about Him is more important than fear. It must be a real belief to gain the achievement of courage.

Borrowed Armor

THERE IS A SPIRITUAL BATTLE TAKING PLACE. BELIEVERS WHO have been saved are in the Lord's army. The Lord gives us spiritual armor to wear to help us against the evil schemes of the devil and his demons. Ephesians 6 contains information about the six different pieces of armor. Imagine, if you will, a metal-armored suit like you will see lining the halls of some castle. What will happen if you throw darts at it? Will the darts stick, or will they bounce off it and fall to the ground?

Much like this metal-armored suit, you can "put on the whole armor of God." This armor is spiritual. It still works even though you can't see it. If someone throws a dart at a store mannequin dressed in clothes and wig, will the dart stick, or will it bounce off and fall to the ground? Without the protective barrier, the dart will get hung in the wig or clothes. The spiritual armor will protect us from the fiery darts of the devil.

There are six pieces of armor that God provides His followers while on the earth:

1. The helmet of salvation
2. The breastplate of righteousness

3. The belt of truth
4. The sword of the Spirit
5. The shield of faith
6. The shoes of peace

The helmet of salvation—This is to help us from the enemy's dart of planting negative thoughts, such as doubt and fear, that affect our minds. We choose what we want to think. We can easily dismiss it or choose to dwell on it. The helmet is to protect our mind.

The breastplate of righteousness—This is to protect our heart and emotions. Emotions are created for the good and a way to experience what God has made. There are times when people or situations are bad, and it has a damaging effect on our emotions. We can choose to acknowledge what has happened and hand it over to God. He is our vindicator. He can repay bad or good in more ways than we ever can, so it is best to let Him handle it. We don't have to pretend it didn't happen, but we can choose to forgive and share our thoughts and feelings to God about it. We don't want a root of bitterness to set in and grow.

The belt of truth—This is at the core of the body. The scriptures contain many truths that will keep us centered and strengthened. Memorizing key verses that we can recite to ourselves to remind us of these truths will help us tremendously. Strengthening the core is essential physically when exercising and works the same way spiritually.

The sword of the Spirit—This movable weapon is an offensive piece as well as defensive. Hebrews 4:12 mentions the

Word of God is sharper than a two-edged sword. When we read and quote the scriptures, it is like wielding the sword in a fight. When we go throughout our day and work toward God's goal for our lives, we can walk on the offense by empowering ourselves with the truths in the Word of God—armed and ready. We can wield this sword when the enemy comes to attack us by refuting his lies using words from scriptures. The only way to know the scriptures is to spend time reading it. Scriptures, praise/worship, and prayer are powerful against the enemy. I don't think many have been taught about the power that exists in those things. If we truly know just how powerful they are, we will use them more often.

The shield of faith—This is a movable piece held up to block the fiery darts of the devil so that your vulnerable parts are protected. Hebrews 11 is popularly referred to as the Faith Hall of Fame among some churches. This chapter in the New Testament portion of the Bible tells us about some of the people who had great faith. Faith is not a feeling. *Faith* is defined in Hebrews 11:1 (KJV) as "the substance of things hoped for, the evidence of things not seen."

Just like walking up to a chair and sitting in it, you use faith that if you sit in it, it will not collapse. You can't see that faith, even though you have seen the chair. You know in your mind that a well-made-looking chair will hold your weight. It is not a feeling, but you somehow know. You have sat in chairs before. You've had a history of sitting in chairs that have held your weight just fine. In much the same way, having faith in God and seeing Him work things out for you and others builds up your faith. The more you see faith work, the more faith you will have for future situations.

A history of faith in God causes great faith. When the enemy tries to attack any part of you, not only do you have that piece of armor but you also have the shield you can hold up. Remind yourself of the times you have used your faith in God and how He has protected you or worked things out. Your back does not have a piece of armor because God's got your back!

The shoes of peace—This piece helps your walking feet carry the Gospel of Jesus Christ. Secure footing is *critical* to keep from falling. Be wise and use this armor provided to you, and this advantage will help you move forward in your Christian life. Build a strong foundation on which to stand by reading the Word of God and committing truths and principles to memory. Familiarize yourself with these. There will be times when you need guidance and direction. There is a preacher from an old country church I have gone to many years ago who has often said, "What's down in the well will come up in the bucket." Have God's Word in your heart and mind so that you have that familiar well of information to draw from in life's circumstances.

We greatly err not knowing the scriptures. You may be under the assumption the devil has more authority than he really has. For example, the gifts we are given at the time of salvation are from the Lord. Spiritual gifts are mentioned in 1 Corinthians 12:4–11 in the Bible. The devil cannot take them. They are ours. But what he will try and do is steal your joy or attack you to the point that you don't feel like using them. He won't have to take them then; he has just tricked you into not using them. Talents are different. You have been born with talent, but spiritual gifts are given at the point of salvation.

Now that you know God has equipped you, you can persevere. Persevering is trying to keep going no matter what your current circumstances are. There is an ebb and flow of life. Push through the hard times and don't quit.

We are never truly alone in our situations. It may feel like it, but God is always with us. Draw closer to God, and He will draw closer to you (James 4:8). Shift your focus from your situation and put it on the Savior.

The enemy will try and whisper thoughts of negativity, discouragement, defeat, despair, and condemnation. Negativity like that does not come from God. Spot that devil! God will convict like, "Don't do that," or "That's not what you should say." Those types of messages are cautions from God because they do not reflect His character. Anything that tries to draw you away from God and cause a separation from your closeness is demonic. Spot the clues!

I know in my life I have found through several experiences that the enemy will reveal itself through his own fear. One good example will be my writing this book. The enemy will whisper, "Yeah, you don't want to write that thing. Who is going to read it? You haven't written a book before; therefore, you have no credibility. Who is going to take anything you say seriously? Yeah, just save yourself the trouble and future embarrassment by just not writing it at all. There are plenty of books already in the world. Who needs yours? You will spend all that time writing, and then no one will read it. This will make you feel horrible, and what a time waster that will turn out to be! Who do you think you are anyways?" How many countless interruptions from the dog, the kids, work, and life have caused me to have to write later? Later becomes much later. The more I try to write, the more things tend to happen to interrupt my writing. Do you notice the tactics?

At first, doubt and fear are presented. Although it sounds logical, the truth is missing. At this juncture, I have a choice. Do I believe in these negative thoughts, or do I dismiss them and continue? This book needs to be written because God keeps pressing on my mind to write it.

Once I dismiss the negativity and continue forward, what comes next? Obstacles. The more I try, the more numerous the obstacles. Why? Because really, the enemy doesn't want a book like this to be written or help anyone. The enemy's fear is someone learning his tactics. So he tries to do whatever is possible to keep it from taking place. He uses simple, everyday things to cause obstacles. The more he tries to work against me, the more I know he is exposing his own fear. If the enemy is afraid of what I am doing, then I am on the right track in doing something for the Lord!

If the enemy is not bothering you, ask yourself why. Does he have the idea you are on the same side? Does he not view you as a threat to his negative work? Self-analyze. The devil can only win if you give up or quit the good fight.

Perseverance

WHEN I WAS LEARNING HOW TO RIDE A BIKE WITHOUT TRAINING wheels, I fell several times, trying to maintain my balance. My father would say, "Well, are you going to lay there and eat the grass, or are you going to get up and try again?" Even though life is hard, and we don't have the ability to master it right away, we can keep trying. We may fall, and that's OK, but we get back up and try again.

Sometimes the knockdown in life is swift and hard. It may take a little bit to get back up. Determine to try again. Don't quit. Don't lay there and eat the grass, so to speak. You've come too far to stop now. The goal is closer now than in the beginning. You can make it through—better is coming! Have hope. Just take a chance and believe. You won't find the better part by staying on the ground. You can do this! Philippians 4:19 tells us we can do all things through Christ, who gives us strength (good verse to keep in your well of information).

Let's define *perseverance*:

> Steadfastness in doing something despite difficulty, failure, or opposition (Lexico.com)

> Persistence in a course of action (Dictionary.com)

> The quality that allows someone to continue trying to do something even though it is difficult (*Merriam-Webster Dictionary*)

Perseverance can be developed. Circumstances will happen in life, and over time, you will become more resilient. Here are a few matters to persevere in:

- Prayer
- Faith
- Situations
- Physical trouble
- Emotional trouble

Think back on some situations where you made it through. At the time, it was tough, but you persevered.

That is just the point, though, isn't it? If you stop, if you give up, you'll never get to finish. You won't see the payoff for your efforts. *I made up my mind. I wasn't going to put all that effort into something, only to stop short, and it would be for nothing.* Even if the progress is small, even if only one small thing is done, that's movement! Sometimes life calls for a pause to rest. Rest, reenergize, and then reboot. All that is useful. Just don't stay there.

Positive and negative self-talk has a lot to do with how far and how long you persevere. Positive self-talk goes a long way. Negative self-talk hinders your progress and presents a defeatist mentality. Look at these two examples:

- **Positive**—"OK, so I messed that up a little bit. But today I am deciding to try again and be a little more focused in my efforts. Yay! I tried again, and I did it!"
- **Negative**- "I can't do anything right. I can't do this. This will never work out for me, so why should I even try?"

Which one do you think is the most helpful? Positive self-talk holds the opportunity to keep going, whereas the negative will lead you to give up.

Celebrating small successes is a way to encourage yourself to continue and realize your progress. After a while, you can look back and see how far you have progressed. Always keep your focus on the short term and the long term.

In 1999, I had a troubled pregnancy and had strange physical episodes. It wasn't until my baby was born that stranger events happened. I was later diagnosed with Hodgkin's disease. I had none of the symptoms. All the things that were going on with me seemed random and unrelated. I was put into one scanning machine after another, and nothing was turning up answers. Happy to at least know something, I started chemo for the first several months of my newborn's life.

We were at a new military duty station, so I didn't know anyone yet. We had not found a church and no family around the area. I had a middle schooler, a toddler, and a newborn. I staged diapers and wipes in different areas of our home and would crawl along the floor during the day to feed and change diapers while my husband was at work and my daughter at school. Chemo made me weak, but I still had to care for the smallest children.

When chemo was finally done and radiation started, my sister-in-law came for about a week or so to cook, clean, and fill my freezer with prepared meals. I was so thankful for her! During those months, though, it was tough to persevere. Thoughts kept entering my mind about not seeing my kids grow up. The enemy took the opportunity to whisper negative thoughts of defeat. At first, I asked the Lord what I did to deserve this. I thought it was a type of punishment.

One night at around two o'clock, I was awake, and with tears in my eyes, I asked the Lord, *Where are You?* I was too sick for the words to come out of my mouth. I prayed with my thoughts.

In my head, I heard a voice saying, *I'm right here. I'm right here. I have not left you.* I cried more because it was so comforting. It was a marked time in my life I would never forget. It took a whole lot of praying through those tears.

I'm so thankful the Lord has heard my cries and prayers and seen me through such a tough time. He has been with me in spirit when I've felt alone. I don't want to know what would've happened if I hadn't persevered. The Lord has used the season of sickness to strengthen my perseverance and faith. He has brought me through to live a 100 percent cancer-free status.

What does this have to do with the Last Days? *Everything.*

That has been one of my seasons. What seasons of life have you been through? The end–times/Last Days are going to be the toughest of them all. The last book of the Bible, Revelation, gives you a glimpse of many events. These past experiences that have made us stronger and more able to persevere have prepared us for what we will have to encounter next.

Significant Books

There are a few significant books mentioned in the Bible that I want to bring to your attention.

- The Book of Truth
- The Book of Remembrance
- The Book of Life

The Book of Truth—In the Old Testament book of Daniel, there was a man named Daniel who was very disciplined with his love and faithfulness to God. If you took time to read through this book, you would get drawn into the different stories of this man's life. His love for God went to the "no matter what" level of dedication. Since he was found trustworthy time and again, God used him greatly.

At around chapter 8, Daniel had another vision. This vision was prophetic in nature and wound up being very specific and at moments very unusual. I could only imagine what he felt as he saw these seemingly strange and profound visions that desperately needed interpretation. What did they all mean?

Here, we read about the angel Gabriel from Daniel's point of view. It is easy to get drawn in by the way it is written.

Daniel 8:26–27 (NASB) says, "And the vision of the evenings and mornings which has been told is true; but keep the vision secret, for it pertains to many days in the future. Then I, Daniel, was exhausted and sick for days. Then I got up again and carried on the king's business; but I was astounded at the vision, and there was none to explain it."

Daniel started to pray, and while he was still talking, here came Gabriel, flying into the scene quickly. Gabriel proceeded to tell Daniel that he was treasured by God and would give him understanding and insight. Then Gabriel told Daniel about 70 weeks. This didn't mean 70 actual weeks but 70 times 7 in terms of years. So we were looking at 490 years having significance. So 483 of these years (69 weeks times 7) would start by restoring and rebuilding Jerusalem and then spanning through time to the Messiah's coming, crucifixion, burial, and resurrection. Once this part was fulfilled, the prophetic clock seemed to stop ticking. This left us one last week, which was referred to as the 70th week.

The last portion of Daniel chapter 9 jumped into talking about the tribulation and the Antichrist. The Antichrist coming on the scene would start the 70th week. At the end of that chapter, the Antichrist would make deals and promises, which the population accepted. Halfway through the 7 years, at the 3½-year mark, a bait and switch took place, and he started doing many horrible things. He would act like he was God but then desecrated the temple. Persecution of Christians would take place, and the only way to buy or sell would be to accept the mark of the beast (666). The worst of times that the world had ever seen would take place. The Antichrist would feel like he could do whatever, whenever, and however. Crime would run rampant. But he didn't get away with it all. Spoiler alert: The Lord would come back and put a stop to him and pour out heavy judgment.

The Book of Truth isn't explained too much in these chapters, but one thing is very certain: If an archangel of the Lord comes to visit you, be alert and listen to what is being told. Have some respect. The angel has come for a reason, and the truth needs to be heard. Messenger angels have delivered words to people at certain times throughout the Bible.

Other signs to note will be unusual weather, famine, and bread that costs a day's wage. Jumping over into the New Testament side of the Bible, we see in Luke 21:8–28 that the 70th week of Daniel is mentioned again. In this passage, my Bible version has the Lord's words written in red letters. This passage is right from the Lord's mouth. He mentions events that have already happened, those that have not yet happened, and those to be aware of that will happen.

So how close are we until Jesus comes for His own? Very close! Look at what has already happened. Look at what is currently happening in the world today. Can we know when exactly? The answer is given in Matthew 24:36–44: just be ready.

There are some signs to watch for (Luke 21):

1. Nations rising against nations
2. Great earthquakes in different places

3. Famines
4. Pestilences (such as COVID-19)
5. Great signs from heaven (sky)
6. Persecution and betrayal
7. Jerusalem being surrounded by armies

Recently in the news, the wars in Ukraine and Israel and military exercises taking place very close to Taiwan are a few of the military unrests in today's world.

There are a couple of YouTube channels that I watch for global weather events. If you don't watch it somewhat frequently, you will not be aware of the global catastrophic weather that has been taking place. I watch in amazement and understand how famine will be coming. The number of global earthquakes is well over 500–600 daily. The most I have been shown is over 850. It fluctuates all the time, but significant activity is taking place.

As a result of the floods, mudslides, heavy hailstorms, and droughts in different global locations, how are we going to have crops to buy when they have been destroyed all over the world? Let's talk about food prices going up. Revelation 6:6 mentions 2 lb. of wheat for a day's wage and 6 lb. of barley for a day's wage. How much do you earn in a day at work? Do you want to pay that much for bread?

I had seen on the news locusts, june bugs, and swarms of insects destroying crops. We experienced COVID-19, a microscopic enemy we couldn't even see, and it shut the world down. Everyone was going through periods of shutdowns and quarantines. Thousands of people lost their lives while thousands of others experienced fear and anxiety.

Look to the skies. Have you seen anything unusual? Some of the YouTube global weather channels have shown doorbells or security cameras capturing balls of light soaring through the night skies in different parts of the world. This has happened on several occasions in the last few months. Large solar flares cause radio blackouts from the magnetic disturbances. Keep looking.

Next are persecutions and betrayals as well as the armies surrounding Jerusalem. Keep an eye on the times.

One day a worldwide trumpet will sound. Christ will return in the sky and rapture up all the ones who have accepted Him as their personal Lord and Savior. The dead will rise first and then the living. Those not raptured will be left behind and experience a time of tribulation. Many events in the tribulation will go from bad to worse. The tribulation will last for 7 years. The first half (3½) won't be as bad as the last half. After the 7 years are over, Christ's Second Coming (where He steps foot on the earth) will take place with an all-ending battle of Armageddon.

The Book of Remembrance—We keep photos to remember specific people and events that are significant to us (some more than others, but we keep them). We store them on our phones, tablets, and even old-school photo albums. We keep high school or college yearbooks and even grade school pictures of our early years. These help us remember. The Book of Remembrance is mentioned in the Bible as where the acts of kindness and other deeds are recorded. See Malachi 3:16–18.

My *abuela* (*grandma* in Spanish) was a kind and generous woman. She would sacrifice deeply for her family and gave to strangers and friends. She was always willing to help if it was in her power to do so. The list would be too great to record everything I saw her do, as well as the unseen, had I witnessed it. She was my life's example. I'd always remember her for her love and generosity. She cared enough to help us think through processes and gave us guidance. She helped us realize the principle of cause and effect as much as possible.

Every deed has a seed in it. Every seed turns into a harvest. Good seeds produce good harvests or good results, and bad seeds have bad harvests or bad results. Obadiah 1:15 speaks about deeds coming back on your head. You know the old saying "What goes around comes around"? That will be like the modern version of this principle.

The Book of Remembrance is a documentation of our deeds. Hebrews 6:10 (KJV) says, "For God is not unrighteous to forget your work and labor of love, which ye have shewed towards His name, in that ye have ministered to the saints, and do minister." Matthew 25:31–46 is a passage where we see that our actions are noticed and that reward or judgment will be given accordingly. We are given a valuable tip in Matthew 6:19–21 (KJV): "Lay not up for yourselves treasures upon earth, where moth and rust doth corrupt, and where thieves break through and steal; But lay up for yourselves treasures in heaven, where neither moth no rust doth corrupt, and where thieves do not break through nor steal. For where your treasure is, there will your heart be also." By this, we see that working to gain treasures on the earth will not amount to anything when you die or when this world comes to an end. You can't take any of it with you. What will you have? The wise thing to do will be to lay treasures in Heaven. So what will that include?

A few examples are showing kindness, whether others show it back or not, giving to others without expecting anything in return, volunteering at church, telling others about Jesus and showing love as His hands and feet, and sharing the good news of the Gospel. Don't go around broadcasting your good deeds. It is easy to put it on social media or to brag about it, but the biggest test will be to do it secretly or unadvertised. Matthew 6:3 (NKJV) says, "But when you do a charitable deed, do not let the left hand know what your right hand is doing."

My kids have watched and participated in giving. Teaching children to give while they are young will produce adults who are giving because the way of life has been established. Teaching children to see and fill a need trains them to take the focus off themselves and be aware of what is going on around them. Teaching the next generation to be givers and not takers is essential. Let them learn by example how to lay up for themselves treasures in Heaven. Help them start that! Hebrews 6:10 tells us that God is not unjust to forget our deeds and love we have shown others.

The Book of Life—This book refers to Jesus Christ, the Lamb of God, who is the sacrifice to pay for our sins. His blood has been shed for everyone. Those who choose to accept this gift of salvation belong to God. Their names are recorded here. Those who do not choose to accept Jesus Christ as their personal Lord and Savior, then, according to Revelation 20:15, will be thrown into the lake of fire. They will never be able to leave from there.

If you start reading at the beginning of that chapter or zoom in around verse 11, you will see there will be a "great white throne" judgment for the ones rejecting Jesus Christ's gift of salvation. In a very big contrast to that situation, there will be a very different kind of event for those who choose to believe and accept salvation. This is the judgment seat of Christ. This is mentioned in Romans 14:10–12. We learn that it is not God the Father but God the Son (Jesus Christ) who will be the Judge from the passage John 5:22. It seems fair to me that Jesus Christ will be the Judge since He has sacrificed so much. Those believers judged at the bema seat will receive rewards for their actions done for Christ (2 Corinthians 5:10).

How you want this to play out is only good while alive on the earth. Will you choose Jesus or reject Him? This is the one and only deciding factor. Jesus is the *only* way to Heaven. John 14:6 (NKJV) says, "I am the way, the truth, and the life. No man comes to the Father but through me." God won't send you to Hell. You will send yourself by rejecting Jesus's blood sacrifice, which is payment for your sins. You choose. What do you stand to face later? Which judgment will you face? You *will* be at one of them. We know this because He tells us in Romans 14:11 (KJV) that we will all answer up. "As I live, says the LORD, every knee shall bow to Me, and every tongue shall confess to God."

Let it be a good event and not a bad one. You will still have the chance now to make your eternal investment. What will it be? Please choose Christ and work toward deeds that will lay up for yourselves treasures in Heaven. Time is running short. Once you leave this world, there are no more chances. If little has been laid up, your eternity will have that amount. If a lot is laid up, your eternity will have that amount. If you find yourself realizing that you are headed for the great-white-throne judgment, the time is now to accept Jesus Christ as your personal Lord and Savior. Only He can pay the payment for your sins. There is nothing you can ever do to pay for it yourself. Sin is not allowed in Heaven. There is only one way. You can receive this gift today by saying this prayer:

> Jesus, I know I am a sinner, and there is no way I can pay my sin debt myself. You died on the cross and shed Your blood as payment for my sins. You were buried in a tomb and rose again on the third day. You live now and will come back for all those who are Yours. I accept, believe, and confess this and ask You to come into my heart as my personal Lord and Savior. Thank You for Your love, grace, and mercy. In Jesus's name, amen!

If you prayed this prayer, welcome to the family of God! Reach out to your local Bible-believing church and share the good news of this life-changing decision. Become part of a local family of believers so you can grow stronger in your Christian walk.

Post-Rapture

THE END-TIME IS A SPECIFIC SERIES OF EVENTS. IT IS NOT AN unorganized mixture of random chaos. If you find yourself still here after the Rapture, you can still choose Christ and work to tell others. You still have a chance to make it to Heaven. Read the book of Revelation (last book of the Bible). The New American Standard Bible will have wording that is more understandable.

Crisis after crisis will be taking place. Don't let hopelessness and fear take over. There are some efforts you can do, and knowledge is empowering. Since many of the true believers in Christ (Christ followers) are not around anymore to mentor you, literature and videos will need to take their place. There is a learning curve. If you find that the economy has crashed, you may not have the internet. If you still have internet, I have three recommendations for you to search: Craig Groeschel from Life Church, Dr. Charles Stanley from In Touch Ministries, and Dr. John Hagee from Cornerstone Church (San Antonio, Texas). These are the three pastors the Lord has led me to mention here. You will learn good, solid teaching, guidance, and encouragement from them. You can find their messages on video and social media platforms as well as their websites. If internet is no longer available, DVD, CD, or literature will need to be your resources. With this information, not only will you feel helped but others will also. These three pastors have key things you will find very useful. I urge you to strongly consider listening, watching, or reading as much as possible. This will be to your advantage.

Let's go over some practical concepts. If thousands have suddenly disappeared, then traffic and other accidents have taken place. Do you need medical care? You may want to go sooner rather than later as the hospitals will get overwhelmed.

Try to find others that you know. Can you locate any family or friends? Do you see any coworkers? You will want to locate someone familiar to avoid feeling alone during this chaotic time. Anxiety will be very high.

Even though Christ followers have disappeared, that doesn't mean doom yet for you. The Lord will return a second time. It's still not too late to accept Jesus Christ as your personal Lord and Savior.

Do not take any mark the world leaders will want everyone to get. To buy or sell, a specific mark will become required. This is the mark of the beast. Essentially, it marks you as Satan's property. Christ followers are not to receive this mark. Try to find a group with which to barter to get your needs, or stockpile before this marking event. Do you have a skill set that you can use to barter? You can trade work done in exchange for something you need.

There will be two groups of people during this time. There will be those who follow the Antichrist and those who will become Christ followers. New Christ followers will need to unify and become self-sufficient now. Unifying with other Christ followers will provide strength and comfort as you navigate through the next seven years of tribulation. Hope will make a tremendous difference.

Your New Job

THERE IS A NEW JOB FOR YOU TO DO DURING THESE NEXT SEVEN years. There is an unseen time clock counting down the remaining time. You can't see nor hear that it is ticking time down, but it is. These years are the last remaining chance to accept Christ as your personal Lord and Savior. When the time clock runs out, the chances are gone and your eternity chosen.

Help others to come to know Christ. You can do this! Start by talking about *your* story. It is a good starting point. The more you share how you have become a Christ follower, the easier you can show how they can too. Tell them how they can accept Jesus as their Lord and Savior, as explained in this book. There will be people rejecting this. Some will act harshly toward you. There will also be people who will accept Christ, and you will have influenced their eternity. You will want someone to do that for you, right?

Trying your best in this effort is your greatest mission right now. When you have days that are not great, find your comfort, strength, and hope in Jesus. The Bible teachings and explanations provided is how God speaks to us. We speak to Him when we pray. Pray! Pray to God as if He is sitting near you. You can whisper it, or you can pray with your thoughts. You can pray in a group. Each of your prayers will be said in a way that helps others who don't know how to pray or feel stuck in knowing what to say in prayer. Make the effort to build knowledge and relationships through prayer.

Praise and worship music does a lot as well. It lifts your spirit, makes you feel understood, and soothes you in a special way. Music is expressive. Each day do your best to take care of the matters you can. Encourage and support one another. Gather frequently.

Next, it will be important to eat as best as you can. Make nutrient-dense foods as a priority. The right foods can be healing. Your health is vital. Hope is crucial.

These will be the toughest of times. Be smart. Be vigilant. Keep the faith. There is a special mention in the Bible about the tribulation saints. This refers to those who have become Christ followers during the tribulation, and some will lose their lives. You can read all about the series of events in the book of Revelation.

THE SEVEN SEALS

White Horse: Deception	Red Horse: War	Black Horse: Famine	Pale Horse: Pestilence ¼ die	Martyrdom & Great Tribulation	Heavenly Signs		
1st Seal	2nd Seal	3rd Seal	4th Seal	5th Seal	6th Seal	SILENCE IN HEAVEN Rev 8:1-6	7th Seal
Rev 6:1-2	Rev 6:3-4	Rev 6:5-6	Rev 6:7-8	Rev 6:9-11	Rev 6:12-17		

THE SEVEN TRUMPETS

⅓ grass & trees burned	⅓ sea blood ⅓ ships and sea life destroyed	⅓ water turned bitter	⅓ sun, moon and stars do not shine	"Locusts" wield Beasts miliary power	2M army ⅓ man killed	Kingdom of God declared
Rev 8:7	Rev 8:8-9	Rev 8:10-11	Rev 8:12	Rev 9:1-12	Rev 9:13-21	Rev 11:15-19

THE SEVEN BOWLS

1st	2nd	3rd	4th	5th	6th	7th
Sores on men with Mark of beast	Sea of blood All creatures die	Rivers, waters turn to blood	Man scorched by sun. Blasphemes God	Beasts seat afflicted	Euphrates dies up. Armies gather to Armageddon	Earth is utterly shaken
Rev 16:2	Rev 16:3	Rev 16:4-7	Rev 16:8-9	Rev 16:10-11	Rev 16:12-16	Rev 16:17-21

The following world events can be monitored:

A. The seven seals

1. The crowned horseman riding a white horse arrives to conquer the earth.
2. The sword-wielding horseman riding a red horse arrives to cause war and take peace from the earth.
3. The horseman carrying a pair of scales riding a black horse arrives to make food scarce.
4. The horseman called Death rides a pale horse, with Hades following him. Together, they kill a quarter of the earth by sword, hunger, beast-attacking people, and death.
5. The martyrs cry to the Lord for justice. They will be given white robes to wear and will rest until a specific number of believers have been killed.
6. There are natural disturbances. The sun turns black, the moon turns red, stars fall from the skies, the skies open like a scroll, and mountains move from where they are. Fear strikes everyone.
7. Silence in Heaven for thirty minutes is the pause before the seven trumpets.

B. The seven trumpets

1. Hail and fire mixed with blood will be thrown to the earth, killing all grass and a third of trees.
2. One-third of sea life and ships get destroyed by a mountain-like fire that is thrown into the sea, causing a third of the waters to turn to blood.

3. The star Wormwood falls to Earth, causing a third of the water to become bitter and making people die.

4. A third of the sun, a third of the moon, and a third of the stars darken, causing day and night to be disrupted. Then an angel flies through the sky, warning everyone about the events that follow each of the last three trumpets. This will be bad.

5. The angel with the key that unlocks the bottomless pit will release locusts that sting like scorpions, which will torment anyone without the seal of the Lord on their foreheads. The torment will last for five months.

6. The four angels bound in the Euphrates River are released, and they will kill a third of mankind. After the two witnesses are taken up to Heaven, the seventh trumpet will sound.

7. This trumpet announces the imminent Second Coming of Jesus. God's temple in Heaven opens, followed by earthquakes, lightning, thunder, and severe hail.

C. The seven bowls

1. It is poured out, giving terrible-smelling and painful sores on all who have the mark of the beast and worship his image.

2. It is poured on the sea, killing all sea life.

3. It is poured on rivers and springs, turning the waters to blood.

4. It is poured on the sun, and men were scorched with heat and cursed God.

5. It is poured on the beast's throne, and his kingdom falls into darkness, causing anguish and self-mutilation.

6. It is poured on the Euphrates River, and it dries up, making a path for the armies to meet at Armageddon. This will be a war to end all wars.

7. It is poured out into the air, and the greatest earthquake in the history of man takes place. The largest hail ever falls along with lightning and thunder. People still curse God.

Look in anticipation for the Second Coming of Jesus Christ! Keep the anticipation of it in the forefront of your mind. He's coming back for you and other Christ followers! Do all that you can in the meantime. There will be a great battle of Armageddon, and that is the final war. It is a showdown between good and evil. Judgment will rain down on the wicked, and the righteous will be vindicated. The Lord has always said that vengeance is His, and He will repay. Then comes a millennium reign where there will be no evil, no Satan for us to deal with. If there were ever a utopian time, this would be it.

After one thousand years, another showdown will happen, and the devil will be chained to the floors of Hell forever. You can remind him of that too! There will be a marriage supper of the Lamb in Heaven. Things too glorious to describe will take place there. Saved Christians will see and be reunited with those who have passed away. I look forward to seeing my brother and *abuela* again!

I hope to speak to you in Heaven someday. May the Lord bless and keep you.

The Extras:
Get-Me-by Homemade Stuff

DON'T YOU JUST DREAD SPENDING MONEY AT THE GROCERY store on stuff that you can't even eat, but it makes the total rise quite a bit when you get to the checkout? Me too. So this is why I have started searching for ways to cut down on that quite a bit so that money spent on overpriced laundry liquid and such can be better used. Here are some solutions to that problem.

Making your own can keep the quality while cutting the cost dramatically. If you have any questions or concerns or any medical conditions, always consult an appropriate professional first. The following is simply what my family has done, and we are sharing ideas with you. These items are available in America, but you may have something similar products where you are.

Laundry Detergent

This recipe will make ten gallons cheaply.

Ingredients

1. Bright yellow box of washing soda (not the orange box of baking soda).
2. White box of borax.
3. Bar of soap. Here, you have a choice. You can use a laundry bar such as Fels-Naptha or Zote, or you can use a bar of soap with a fresh smell like Zest, a lavender-scented bar of soap, or castile bar soap. (Castile soap will make a smoother liquid.)
4. Buckets (two five gallons should work, not unless you want to divide it some other way). Buckets with handles are preferred for easier moving.
5. Large pot that is not used at all for food. I got one at the thrift store just for this purpose.

Out of all this supply, you will be able to make several batches of laundry liquid. If you take the total cost of this and divide it by how many batches you will be making, you can see how much cheaper it is to make your own.

Instructions

Put a large pot of water to boil (about a gallon).

Grate the bar soap with a cheese grater. I get one from the thrift store and keep it as part of my soapmaking supplies. This way, it doesn't get used to risk contamination. Put in a large blender. I got one from the thrift store for the same reason as the grater. If the blender isn't a large-capacity one, you may have to blend things in smaller quantities. So perhaps start with half the amount you have grated and save the rest for another blending batch.

Measure one cup of washing soda. For batch blending, only use half right now.

Measure half a cup of borax and do the same. Be careful not to let this get on your skin during this dry state. If it gets on you, just rinse it off.

Your blender should have half portions of soap, soda, and borax. Turn the blender on and shake it around a little bit until everything is blended into a powder form. Try not to have any large pieces. Once everything is blended to a powder form, pour into the large pot of water. Stir and heat until the powder has dissolved. Once it is dissolved, pour half into each bucket.

If you have used a scented soap bar, you will enjoy that smell in your laundry liquid. If you do not use scented soap, you can pour essential oils in this liquid once it has completely cooled. Plain is good too.

You should have two buckets with the soap solution in the bottom of each one. Take each bucket and fill it to handle height. If your buckets do not have handles, then fill it to the largest protruding rim (about two to three inches from the top). Stir the whole time you are adding water. Once both buckets are filled, set aside and give it another stir in the next hours.

How big your family is or how often you wash will determine how long this will last you. You will only need to use about half a cup of this solution for your laundry and one cup for heavily soiled. Always use proper water levels when washing since there needs to be some ability for movement while washing.

Toothpaste

You can learn a lot by reading online and then deciding what you are willing to go through or not for your own toothpaste. Some things I read and thought, *I don't know about all that!*

Other things I read, I thought, *That's too extra!* Then I decided I would take a little bit of this idea and a little bit of that and do an experiment of my own. I was going to be the guinea pig, so I figured, why not?

Please consult an appropriate professional first if you have any conditions or concerns. This is what I have decided on in the end:

Ingredients

1. Organic cold-pressed coconut oil in a jar. Any pesticide in the mouth is not a good idea.
2. Magnesium in powder form. I use Natural Vitality Calm, and the flavor I like is lemon raspberry, but they have others.
3. I use pink Himalayan salt or Redmond Real Salt. I switch between the two, depending on what I have at the time.
4. Mint leaves or a mint tea bag.

Instructions

Put the jar of coconut oil in a window and let it warm up to a liquid. Stick the mint leaves or mint tea bag in the jar and close the jar. Let it sit so that the mint will infuse with the coconut oil for about two weeks. Please plan for this toothpaste.

The more oil you use, the more salt and magnesium you will need. The combination of the three makes a paste that can be stored in a jar or whatever you have. It is up to you to make as much or as little as you like. There is a small scoop inside my magnesium jar. I usually use one scoop of magnesium and half a teaspoon of salt and slowly pour in the oil while mixing until I get the desired consistency.

With this toothpaste, your gums and teeth receive nutrients that will keep you from having dental issues. Now this will not keep you from having *any* dental issues but will significantly reduce the risk. And as a bonus, you can either rinse out your mouth with water or spit most of it out only for lasting protection. It is all healing, so it won't hurt you to have residue. Try to floss before brushing.

Paper Products

Did you know that buying paper products such as toilet paper and paper towels in commercial bulk is cheaper than what you pay in the store? I have been doing this for years. We only use paper plates and cups when we have adverse weather conditions that leave us without power. It is cheaper to wash dishes.

Outdoor Cooking Station

We are building an outside cooking station with cinder blocks and bricks. This way, we can cook outside when it is hot and avoid making the air-conditioning work extra. When it is mildly cold, sometimes being by the fire in the evening is a treat as we sit around it.

Gardening Bed

Did you know that some small plastic swimming pools are made with the same plastic as milk jugs? At least the ones where I live are. You know the small ones that go on sale when spring comes around? Research your area. We can fill them with dirt and use them for gardening beds. Just make sure to make a small hole in the bottom for drainage. Growing your own food from the seeds of food you have already purchased will greatly help. These plastic pools can be set up on tables for easy access. They can be on apartment balconies and backyards. These are mere suggestions. Always use caution and be careful not to do anything that can result in harm.

Apple Cider Vinegar

You may have passed by this in the store countless times not even knowing all the powerful benefits that can come with using apple cider vinegar. It helps with digestion, it cleans your organs, cleans and heals skin wounds, it has relieved my headaches, and it strips off pesticide from your fruits and vegetables. The one with the mother in it is the best form to buy. Look at the bottom of your bottle. If you see some sediment settled at the bottom, that is not spoiling or turning old. That is the good part called the mother. Make sure to shake up your bottle each time you plan on using it.

Side note: much like passing by this without realizing its power, we can pass by our Bibles without realizing the power that is written in the pages. The Lord's Prayer is a powerful example among many. "Our Father, Who are in Heaven, Hallowed be thy Name. Thy kingdom come; Thy will be done on Earth as it is in Heaven. Give us this day our daily bread and forgive us for our trespasses as we forgive those who trespass against us. And lead us not into temptation but deliver us from evil [we all want evil to stay away from us] for thine is the kingdom and the power and the glory forever, Amen." This prayer shows up in a few different places in the New Testament portion of the Bible. One place is Matthew chapter 6. Food for thought.

Wipes

Buy the blue roll of paper towels in the automotive section of a store. This is heavyweight paper and can be washed and reused. Cut the roll in half and place them in plastic containers (maybe empty wipes containers) and wet them down with one of these solutions: isopropyl alcohol (clear or fresh green mint) or vinegar that has been soaked in orange peels or lemon peels.

Garden Insecticide

Growing your own food? Keep pesky, harmful bugs away by peeling an orange or two and boil the peelings in a pot of water for around fifteen to twenty minutes. Let it completely cool. Using a funnel, pour the orange-infused water into a spray bottle. Spray your plants with it to keep bugs away every week. You can also use this as mosquito repellent on your own skin. Use the leftover boiled peels for compost. You can also use lemon balm, but use this as soon as you mix it because it will mold if left unused. Adding lavender does not have a desired outcome.

Survival Bread

Times being what they are, sometimes cutting back is necessary. What you don't want to do is cut your nutrition in the process. This bread is full of intentional ingredients that, when mixed, will provide all the protein, fiber, carbs, and vitamins your body can successfully survive on during hard times. It has complete nutrition.

I've found a recipe online but realized quickly that it isn't really all that desirable. I've wound up making some adjustments because I don't want to feel like I am eating cardboard-flavored bread. If I need to survive on it, I should like it. Feel free to make some tweaks of your own depending on what you have available. If you have any food allergies or medical conditions, adjust accordingly.

Ivonne O. Pyke

Ingredients

¼ cup dry lentils

52 dry kidney beans

80 dry pinto beans

65 northern beans

½ cup raw honey

2 eggs

½ cup oil (olive, coconut, or your choice)

½ cup chopped fruit of your choice (optional)

4 cups warm water (not hot)

1 tsp real salt

2 packets of active dry yeast

2½ cups soft or hard white wheat berries

1½ cups sprouted spelt

½ cup hulled barley

¼ cup millet

The whole grain is best for these, but if you already have it ground up into flour, then use that. Otherwise, these whole forms will need to be ground up finely in either a food mill or a coffee grinder. The dry beans will also need to be ground into a flour consistency.

Instructions

Combine the yeast, warm water, honey, and oil together and let it sit for about five minutes.

Mix dry ingredients into the yeast mixture and let it sit for another ten minutes.

Pour the mixture into your greased loaf pans or your desired baking container and then place it in a warm place for an hour to rise. You can put sesame seeds or pumpkin seeds on top if you prefer.

Now it is ready to bake in an oven preheated to 350°F and check it in forty-five minutes to see if it is done. If not, keep checking every five minutes until a toothpick comes out dry. Let the bread cool completely. Wrap the bread in plastic wrap, Ziploc bag, or whatever you have and store in the refrigerator and freeze the extras.

I hope you can try these suggestions and maybe come up with something of your own. Pioneers had to have a way of making things way back in the day. Think about how something can be made and try to make it yourself.

Be kind. Share when you can. Help when you can. The world can always use a little more kindness.

Notes to Self

Printed in the United States
by Baker & Taylor Publisher Services